S0-CEZ-829

TO ANACREON IN HEAVEN AND OTHER POEMS

FLOOD EDITIONS   CHICAGO

GRAHAM FOUST

TO ANACREON IN HEAVEN AND OTHER POEMS

Copyright © 2013 by Graham Foust. All rights reserved. Published by Flood Editions. floodeditions.com. ISBN 978-0-9838893-5-9. Design and composition by Quemadura. Cover collage: John Stezaker, *Mask VII*, 2005, courtesy of The Approach, London. Printed on acid-free, recycled paper in the United States of America. This book was made possible in part through a grant from the Illinois Arts Council.

YOU OPEN YOUR MOUTH AND A TRADITION
DRIBBLES OUT. —ROBERT POLITO

TO ANACREON IN HEAVEN

AND OTHER POEMS

FRONT MATTER

"To weep into stones are fables."

Sir Thomas Browne wrote that.

"Mark you: the darkness is always a matter of one's own self-contained, severed head."

That's from Thomas Bernhard's *Frost*.

And sometimes a life is that that head becomes selfish, its tongue as thin and bitter as a blade of just-fertilized grass.

A sheet of plywood is a picture of a tree.

And now, thanks to an hour of morning sleep—a small erasure in my day—and a faint dot of pain from a flu shot, I'm all body.

Behind a boarded storefront window, seas of rooms float up, not going everywhere.

INHABITER

New hums in this room, new bones.

Of all the things of which you've never once thought, the ways in which this child could die and this sentence might end can't now be said to be among them.

The color of misremembering is that of a field at evening's edge, a field where you weren't born and you don't live but somehow have to.

Hard by the world and its at-risk trappings, its shit-handed crashes in what can hardly be called miniature, you once went rolling around lonelily, a hole in all you weren't, and even walked on into the woods and didn't get leaves all over you.

Most impossibly close and uncontrollably quiet, your skin's now shadow, your insides a parliament of largely unseen meat.

You scratch a bug bite.

Its itch is knowledge doing something else's job.

TEN NOTES
TO THE MUSE

Every angel's not that bad, actually, but so much as a click from whatever it is you're trying to sing with's total lunacy.

Point being, you're around here somewhere, maybe crouched and for the most part untouched amid well-photographed debris.

I've never met or lived without you.

Hissing my kid to sleep I'm not the sea.

And yet earlier today I was as if poured onto beachfront real estate.

A talk-shaped day, though not a single face came of it.

Rousseau's *War* doesn't hang in the Louvre.

Some nights, half an inch or so from sleep—if that's in fact how such a distance might be measured—I twitch and time goes sideways.

I think I'd live there if I could, and when I'm there I think of you.

Thanks to me we're lost in unison.

Thanks to you I can move without meaning to.

If I could, I'd sing everything you sing to me to you.

I searched the beach for a rock of good shape and you didn't.

I'm so boring I could do it all day but you're worse.

You can hurry love and you do.

In addition to being grief thrown down and into pattern, a poem is as legal as a sculpture of a switchblade; belief's a thought thought true.

I googled myself this morning, and twenty-three screens in I read about one Graham Foust of Junction City, Kansas, whose twenty-five-year-old daughter and her boyfriend were shot dead in their home in Wichita on November 26th, 2009.

And what do you do but help me spit up a line like, "That late in the fall, the Midwest might've had a little yellow left in it."

And to think I wanted something for his trouble, mine.

I flicked a wasp from my juice glass—you said to write it down.

A hairbrush washed up at my feet—I wrote it down.

No time like the future save for most of it.

I cried awhile and crawled into my unspilled head and sat there.

I tossed a balsa-wood glider at a fire.

Days your voice is the house; days the house is the house; days it wouldn't be so wise to state my case—there must be others.

Color-free light on a blueblack garden, say; a single wall in a mostly empty place.

If ever I make a mountain, it's a good bet I'll make it out of sentences with which you'll assist me.

If ever I build a boat, it's a good bet I'll build it out of holes.

The grass smelled like history—you could've told me that.

A broken willow put its branches there—you showed me.

Dear Bob, I once walked home from Cato's with one eye completely closed.

The nerves convert the world from world to memory.

It's not enough that I've been made sure of, that one can get sick from a punch line, that speeches underwater are all the same.

Comes upon and at me does your gone-tinged promise.

I had a plane to miss.

Can I buy you some rain?

For the last half an hour, I've been practicing at setting down a cup
of cheap whiskey noiselessly.

Do something about me.

Make it look like a murder.

What if I get what I believe?

I gawk through thin glass and imagine sounds where I can see them.

What if I were all but one word?

Birds in the cold and some pill-colored clouds and an Airbus is other people.

Tonight's equal parts black and pats of blood behind my eyelids, while other blood winds through me on its rounds.

I was after my own heart; I found a mirror or three.

"Matter," as in "What's the?"

"Spirit," not as in "That's the."

You look like no one else; you look like smoke; I look like me.

Looks don't count for much, I know—it's what's inside that fails.

Problem with poetry's nobody's lonely anymore.

What if I were all one word?

This was an instant message called "And Tall and of a Port in Air,"
and I'm as close to you as I am to total dark when dark's the case.

At faucet, thoughts and water.

Every poem's a failed palindrome.

I fall through ideas as through flowers.

I fall through ideas as through ice.

Was a time when I wanted only dark the whole way down, and now I'm choosing not to think about it that way why?

Any theory craves itself.

Was that a leaf in the overhead compartment?

Reason's at the kidney of the dream.

I recall more dreams than days it seems, and in dreams, days, your kind'll feed me to the keyholes.

Was in a basement conquering atlases.

Was in an attic putting money on a god.

Six and some-odd miles from anonymity, I was no painting, no poem, but from there I hoped to crush that fang of moon.

Gratuitously beautiful often the moon.

When people die I love them more.

The city gets cheap and then expensive again.

I carry on as if the stars were bits of medicine.

If ever you quit me, please know that I'll be dumb and in love with boredom.

Boredom works in obvious ways.

I taught a newborn night because the night was all she knew.

I make these phrases flaws the days fall from and into.

Who'd behead me if on Christmas morning I'm the king of waking?

I made for filth and you were there.

I made for filth but you were there.

A sled in ashes, words in action, the facts and/or the last thing up my mind.

I close both eyes and a piece of movie plays, a clip of me using my teeth to pull the mitten from the hand I'm going to need to pull the staple from the other.

I know of klieg lights in the trees, a little lake like I could pick it up and break it.

Formless, but possible—that's all tomorrow's problem.

I know of klieg lights in the trees because they're there.

If my tongue's in the present, I can taste another tense; as for the past, I'll have the first half, the rest of it, whatever else I get.

A poem's an empty lemon in the mouth of a crow on a phone line.

Oh there you are, that's right—wave like you've done me a favor.

You put a spell on me because I'm never mine.

Midnight and the kid's still breathing.

In the main of place, my own brain around a body, the future falls up like blood.

Got leftover makeshift flakes on the indoor-outdoor.

Thought salmon-colored muscle over bright and unimaginary-bone.

And for my next city trick, I'll think the leaves from the edge of the alley.

I'll mop a floor a couple stories in the air.

For what it's worth, anywhere's the end or the beginning of the earth.

Some *flâneur* came by earlier and tired of himself, and almost no one thought to notice him or care, and that's no shame.

A painter runs two hands through piles of color on a canvas.

The ocean's over there; the eye's a drain.

I'll do what you want or be a moth on water, and when I'm all in these pieces I'm okay with the way certain of them seem to've just crumbled into governance.

I point to failure with an artificial noise.

When I want to know what cars looked like in the year of my birth,
I get out Peter Moore's photograph of Richard Serra's *To Encircle
Base Plate Hexagram, Right Angles Inverted.*

Why do I talk to you like I'm dead?

A vision thrown wide of all time, such bogus heroics: collection the
artist.

A pool cue, a pulpit, a gallows: collection the woods.

The artist, the woods, et cetera, et cetera: collection the inevitable
blaze.

Wherever I'm not there's something or someone.

Rousseau's *War*'s in the Musée D'Orsay.

You said to treat myself as an animal would, and I spent the rest of the day wondering if I should flee from or attack me, the rest of the next day wondering if I should eat my young and suck my claws.

You've given me hash marks and capital, returns on my many impediments; I've given you snow, if that, in paper bags.

The fanny packs and cameras really fucked with the Agnes Martins, but they were completely at home in the room of Philip Gustons, thus making me love Guston all the more.

True, the door to the cave could be heavier.

I feel a glad California morning nausea coming on.

Bleed a road for you, would I?

The "again" in the chorus of "Love Will Tear Us Apart" suggests that love might also keep those two together.

It was poetry taught me that purity's a ruse, that impurity's an industry maybe.

I will never understand how flame's a thing.

Here's a little number called "Tears of a Skull," and when I sing it I feel certain I've been thrust into and spun.

If ever you leave, at least go through me.

I pledge allegiance to a picture not yet hung.

Literature has shape; consumption has.

What if I don't get what I believe?

What I remember most about Bret Ellis's *Less Than Zero* are the CliffsNotes to *As I Lay Dying.*

"Why bother?" says a vague and peeling billboard here in Oakland.

You can tell me why and I'll hear sirens.

FROM A MOUTH IN CALIFORNIA (DAYLIGHT SAVINGS VERSION)

Today my morning run felt awful until I was almost finished, and this is also the sentence in which I admit that I never once considered going any farther.

Later, when asked to participate in a thought experiment regarding preferences for my own demise, I chose a cause of death that involves neither panic nor pain, though this may well mean both have set in.

I'll say this much: right now I'm pulling apart a tangerine, and wherever and whatever these clouds were before they were here feels irrelevant in light of my having only now realized that I'd expected something better from the sky.

That, and I'd like more from this minor wind and the leaves it acti-
vates, two sounds that seem to just catch in me briefly and die.

I let my face come open at jokes.

I let my pulse bump me slowly into sleep.

Sometimes I dream I'm playing a video game based on a movie in
which I've been chased.

Hurry down, function—there's still sun on me.

Pain or panic I believe in I can taste.

SONNET

I sing as if I'm eating what I'm singing from a knife.

TO GRAHAM FOUST ON THE MORNING OF HIS FORTIETH BIRTHDAY

There is a town in north Ontario.

But the pre-the-dream weird, the night gone onionskin, was there a place there?

You can't go back to the sandcastle—the sea will have reduced it to a perfect bust of someone.

Filling up on toast, you miss the green, green grass of somewhere else.

In the dream about the class about art—a dream I'm confident you've never had—all the people in the class about art love art.

But what can one do about the real class about art, about the more real people, most of whom have been taught not to love to cry?

A redwood forest is indivisible in fog, but the point at which one first makes out the sounds of one's accent should have a name.

Ache's got a cinematography to it.

A time-lapsed lily unfurls as if in pain.

An irreversible process is one for which nature has such a preference that the reverse process is meaningless.

In any case, what could be meant by the ungrowth of a flower?

Your own outer order, you've come to love that underordered giant inner life.

The living forever part is over.

Today's another one of your last.

There's a staggering happiness to standing in the yard and wearing someone else's clothes, the very same happiness to sitting in the bath and taking someone else's pills.

There's no one more unhappy than a fat kid with a badminton racket.

There's no acquired taste like inner life.

Nothing.

Nothing.

Knock knock knock.

Three touches and thoughts like wind on a puddle of coffee.

Remember how to change a guitar string?

And what could be more punk than family money?

Because you won't be sticking that spoon in your mouth again anytime soon, you can set it on the counter free of worry.

You can finally write that letter—"Dear Mark Rothko: How few light bulbs does it take to change a picture?"

Morning puts its mitts to you, and suddenly one of your shoulders is over the other.

Scars are somewhat difficult to draw.

Neutral wires are white, and hacking at an old gutter with a moving reciprocating saw blade might well knock you off that ladder.

In the difference between almost and never—*check, check*—this is a song called "The Thinking Song."

It's to be sung by someone with hair, or by a senile broker who stumbles around the exchange during moderate to heavy trading only to end up dead in a mound of tabloids.

This is no poem of fossils under dirt, but it was a poem about Henry James and Catullus on foredecks mourning their brothers.

Happy birthday.

Ave atque vale.

The day's brighter after a couple three beers.

Admit that you've thought to yourself that death's a great way of getting out of being here, a minor change in terminology as might arise when something faint and far away becomes a thing that's disappeared.

You complained that last night was like sleepwalking through flames or glass doors—although you weren't sleeping—and your complaints about not sleeping are like complaints about air are like complaints about a stick of chalk in a bowl of cold milk.

Oh *those* old imagined emergencies?

These bleeds?

Tiny hawks of poetry all over you, you sit at screens to punch a book into a world.

There are two kinds of people in it: those who are overly concerned with going to prison and those who should be far more preoccupied with incarceration than they are now.

In time, tomorrow will grow down to you, but it'll feel like it's coming upon you.

In any case, what could be meant by the ungrowth of a Wednesday?

There's nothing sexier than a wounded supermodel leaning on a cane.

The next room itself is entirely there, but what's in it's a figment of recall, a quotation about products in a home.

You've got the pantry packed with glossy locusts, mock immodesty, the look of miles of ice.

[*Vague bump of a distant radio; enter an ocean and the FBI.*]

Come on—come down into the cracked, gray street.

Wouldn't we know it—summer in Oakland: two bent-up umbrellas near a trashcan how?

By an hour whereof we can't speak in the present tense, the dark had melted.

Sun's up humping silhouettes onto asphalt now; sky's mostly the obligatory blue.

The planet's huge with impending sentences, and your plans—of which I must be more than two—are still on view above a plot of bent wheat.

What you do is me: for that I came.

You'll see me leave—that's how you'll know I'll be gone.

This is the last poem you'll ever write.

Oh I'm joking—laugh or don't laugh, tears or not.

Who between the two of us deserves to be cursed with having only to do nothing or good?

Allow me to pull that mouth off.

You and I are one another in the ways the closest whisper might be called a kiss, and here we are—kiss or no kiss, kiss or not—up close and vanished as per standardized desire.

That said, I'm both camera and satellite, so let's cut live now to where it's night to catch crowds rushing out of various overpriced events converting their initial impressions into speech they can't be bothered to commit to memory.

In your sad and American manner, you get as choked up about the collective as you do over the individual.

When it comes to songs, you're up and down for them, whether anthem or unfathomable murmur.

When it comes to poetry, prose is the World Trade Center of language, free verse the Goldman Sachs.

One day the role of me will be played by no one, the role of you by a piece of meat.

Here's the warmed-up chorus: "You sore excuse for penis / You fucking dim Wisconsin ghost."

Odd to be referred to as the real one, yes, but it's not so difficult not to name things: "rain-bright paint"; "some idea of what I've done"; "smudged tobacco on the hospital steps."

There was a time before you'd forgotten those words, which means that at one point your mouth was somewhat warm from having used them.

I've not accused you of repose in a field of unknown results at noon on the first Tuesday of each month, nor have I accused you of suicide, of loving the void so much you thought you'd make another one up, but if you're alive—even if you've achieved complete amnesia—I'd like those words with you.

And if not, just tell me—I've got some perfume.

A little bird hit you.

A little bird hates you.

Would you look at you look from your skull?

You run your eyes down the mirror, my brain all over your face.

My brain all over your face, you run your eyes up the mirror.

Bed's a good place from which to calibrate the future, and while to-day competes for our compliance, you watch a cloud slide over and die for us.

You take your own shapes every time you lie down, rise in segments like some idiot mime.

It's not entirely correct to say that August is like having blood dumped on you, but let's, until we conjure something else.

Far be it from a season or the sun to be here for good.

Far be it from me to go tipping symbols into this thing or to grind it into a gritless paste.

Far be it from a bird to throw open its tree, or from your mind's gray to think upside said bird as fast as you can eat it.

Far be it from an alphabet's bastard sentences to weld away all difference.

Far be it from anyone to really feel a bone before it breaks.

Far be it from that old man to remove his hat in the presence of a lady and keep it off for the rest of his days.

Leave it to you to stuff this poem with dull colloquialisms, why don't I.

The water'd be lovely were it leather.

How often one wants someone toward whom to just bomb, and how infrequently one wants someone at whom to just make faces in the dusk.

Where there's smoke, there might be next to nothing, and how soon the sound of liquor against the bottom of a glass becomes the sound of liquor falling all over itself, of liquid turning around its own word.

One hour's a series of holes in these sounds, and then another hour moves like snow.

Having mistaken the taste of the weather for a mound of breath between your lips, you'll get you one of each of every fruit in hell.

Once you vowed to be better about hygiene, you found you could no longer understand movies without celebrities in them, and if I'm more than happy to spare your hand—you know the breeze could blow your head into it —I'm back to mangle your half of the shadow.

How is it that you're able to hum the theme from *The Dick Van Dyke Show* even though you haven't heard the tune in thirty years?

Remember when you bit off your other hand and threw it at me, thereby saying goodbye?

Time'll tear, as they say, and make legible every scratch.

Did you say something?

Did I?

Although the numbers didn't indicate any real savings, your recent experimentation with gas-saving gadgets gave you a pleasant placebo-charged feeling of success.

How many times do you have to tell us that when it comes to breathing it's all next; that we'll be shamed, really, by our own freak hopes; that one drunk grad student's lost inhaler is another's theory-ridden found poem.

Here—have a figure for the way you're cruel: a mall built to look like what it's replaced, its bits of disingenuous similitude.

The mannered poem could not be a gift, but there have nevertheless been flowers.

Bless you.

Guess what?

Being pissed off and despondent isn't the same as being a total asshole, the vice president, or a misogynist.

The president travels with bags of his own blood.

Would you look at me look from your skull?

The mannered theory could not be a trick, couldn't merely be the theorist hitting the reader on the palate with a little brick.

(This from someone who's been content to think of your switching to water as a miracle.)

On the off chance I were to tell you that you're the axis on which our shared heart spins, would you turn yourself into a harpoon, or could you consider other options?

Before you answer, know that you'll soon be wading out into the afternoon like you're about to pin a medal on someone you hate.

The pleasing is legal—and it should be—but the sublime, in your latest home state, is (I'm sorry) only mandatory.

You go small into its wads of progress.

You knew to learn early what might be meant.

To wit, your dad said to go and get the rifle, and a brief piece of theater commenced.

You moved, gesticulated, talked in a kind of vacuum—the vacuum itself being more interesting (or at least counting for more) than anything that went on inside it.

You: "Where's the rifle?"

Dad: "Check the top shelf of the closet—you'll need the ladder-thing."

You: "Where's the stepstool?"

Dad: "In that painting."

Thought to be there looking through the picture plane into a space, you, Graham Foust, grabbed up a chunk of soft despotism, slopped it on into your mouth, and began to chew.

You chewed as though you were somehow chewing music.

Then you said, "It's like everything never happened."

You said, "I feel; therefore, the one universe just pushed through itself—don't you know, don't you see, isn't that it?" (the two of us still pulling on a door).

Now you're pressure-washing the back patio with a forty-degree nozzle, moving the tip from side to side in a lethargic sweep about a foot or so from the concrete.

Tell me, professor, if you know—what's the sound of one grown man losing his shit in public?

Tell me, professor, if you know—the time.

Begin with a regular alarm clock and remove its hands.

You're left with two concentric shafts rotating at different rates.

These are the new hands.

Remove the shafts.

You're left with gears as the even newer hands.

Remove the gears.

There's no clock.

Come on—let's ride the train for the thousandth time.

I'll let you get that boy of yours to school.

Guy on the other platform'll pull his coat around his cell phone and start to bawl.

I'll let you think you're happier than him.

In the inexact light that must be blurring the shapely hills, the same light that finds you always already "Alright already, alright already," you don't want to get adjusted to this longitude; you're not enough to make it sound like more.

And it's true that you always touch the stuff, that you don't sleep through the proof through the night.

Your daughter's just been born; you're just now forty; and here you are making decisions in terms of the historical sediment of contingencies known as instincts.

Yes, light, there is no other word for it.

Yes, light is speech.

Yes, light.

You weren't quite ten when Joseph Brodsky turned your age.

He wrote about how omelets made him barf.

What else did he say about his own life then?

That it was long and abhorred transparence?

I might say the same thing about this poem.

The more you peel it back to secrets, the more collapsed the whole enterprise looks, the less like poetry the poem seems to be.

There were times I used to think of you as a peep show and not as a person, because I didn't crave most of what you were.

These days, you name it—I'll try to take it all away: your neighbor-
hood, even the ceiling.

But I can never get everything, see?

That house there's almost half full of debris.

The walls are here to walk, the floors to climb, while Earth flies its
white old kite of a moon.

An insomniac is someone for whom waking is more difficult than
it is for other people, whoever *they* are.

The television's full of hissing stars.

Hypnos won't have you—you're become teeth, sweat, skin, teeth,
teeth, and impossibly sore.

To heaven with some priceless ball of dream.

Let this morning be a coin fresh from a forge.

ARS POETICA

Turn your face away and break a first-floor window.

Turn back and throw its pieces through your open one above.

UNCHAINED MELODY

I crawl from autumn's download.

Bad credit's in the air like air.

This morning's bunged abysses, trapped the dreams in—it gets worse; nursed forward, I think to nod my head and it's not there.

Wind scatters leaves from some of these trees around some others.

I stifle every laugh and every cry so as to hear.

TO THE READER

I mean to pry, to fail to gain and know it.

My days are mostly framed before they're painted.

It's never so too late as when the face of a state-murdered person drops its shape, and then the sun comes swallowingly on behind idealess clips of gray.

I could breathe so quickly as to kill myself.

As always, anyone's hands.

THE ONLY OTHER LIFE THEN

In a closet, his body crabbed with fear, he screams not for his life, as that'd be the quiet scream, but for the other life, the loud scream, during which he pulls ties and shirts and coats and pants and hats to the small square floor.

While he's remembering that he can't expect the world to be always hospitable, he digs for air (his clothes've buried him) and as he prepares another scream he thinks of elsewhere in the house, of an expanding room (and dark) evoking well-forgotten lectures from a college course in physics barely passed.

He asks no one in particular if he might not yet be dying; if in a new place he moves with one of these shirts half on his back; if yanking pant legs, unable to get an old jacket around his torso, unbuttoning cuffs and grabbing madly at a fur-lined cap, he's now no prisoner of the customs that rendered them them, him him, their possibilities stretched to where they'll cover nothing else, as if transparency might've been the only other life then, before the dream that someone said to keep before him dropped away.

FOUR SHORT FILMS

From this side, my closed eyes are the colors of bricks without sun on them.

The sea's so windless I may never make it home.

I thought my skin might make a fine spinnaker, but the torn dark form I glommed onto however many hours ago's not going any-where.

Some things I always learn.

Wherever I am's another place on the world from which whoever I could've been's been banished.

Whatever I make myself say that it does, my reflection in this water doesn't "float."

The meaning of my dream is you can't have it.

Alone in the dark at the start of the day, I can tell by the noise of the cars on the road that it's rained.

Or, bundled up and descending a subway staircase, the day done without, another gash in whatever time I might have left to agree with gravity, I recognize someone—but not from where I think I do—and if this is a grief, it's an easy one, a lowish tax that bankrolls my own recent appearances on the oxygen side of the sky.

In either case, a black oval props open my mouth.

Inaccuracy's inevitable, and even sleep is gestural.

Now back to pain in a room lit with teeth.

I suck in my gut while I limp through the real.

It's as if some lovely person stood there, a taser in one hand, a mug of hot-but-not-too-hot broth in the other.

The planet arranges its weather; a garden grows apart and answers water.

No thing I touch—not even the edge of any page—thinks anything of me.

All the more here for its having left the branch, a leaf I mentioned earlier goes scratching down the sand.

Fog like a body bag; a mediocre fire—call this California dismal with a chance of purple flowers.

A nameless face will tend to harden as if in a painting.

Was anything pretty before pictures?

Was everything?

Of what forgotten use is my intending to be empty, my listening hard for what's misunderstood?

Die a couple times—see how you like it.

The light'll be the same here for a while.

PREQUEL

They're lowering me into me.

This is where I came in.

TO ANACREON
IN HEAVEN

AND TO RICHARD DEMING

World without anything, dark without stars—and then the poem,
some imagined glass, half full of its own shards.

(Said world's no less confusing than the sun and no more mine.

The shortest distance between two ideas is fear; the shortest distance between three ideas is pain.

The beginning sang that to belong was noise, and then whole thoughts came coursing through some head's more morbid tributaries.

We killed them, called them "Him," braved information, and in these acts erased entire times of day.

Would that I—and by the way, I know of no square flower—would that I could hear that scrap of twilight rooms away.

In what feels like official evening, there's space to think and maybe to walk in the brass-flavored rain.

Blood in more than one of them, a few photographs perform me; a spider stitches air and lets me look at it.

Remember that the poem, while not used in the language-game of information, is composed in the language of information.

I'm in thin and particular flames.

What I talk about when I talk about nothing—the wind-body prob-
lem.

Italicized every so often by a streetlight, I take my chopped-open
mouth and my time into the night.

Hello there carnivore.

Hello there lizard-half twitching on the asphalt.

The city lake's a conversation, dim juice, its weeds like keywords;
the poem so perturbed, another worry.

Nature poem: "The aforementioned wind brings all the ready-
mades to the lawn."

On one side or another of the glass, an old animal yawns.

Love poem: "She's the first sound the house makes in a power out-
age"; or, "Yes and no for an answer's in the air."

At one side or another of the glass, a young animal stares.

Language poem: "Oh *do*, that dummy modal, no meaning of its own."

On one side or another of the glass, the whole barnyard moans.

I've come straight into the room in which the poem was to be for me.

What with the sun's abbreviation, I might've forgotten to walk around.

I got the dark all wrong, which means I'll get the day all wrong.

There's a corner in my neighborhood that smells like a woman I haven't stood near in fifteen years.

My mother works in a big-box bookstore in a strip mall in the town where I grew up, which means I'm regularly informed when someone with whom I went to high school buys a sexy magazine.

The whole process is a mess.

What a little moonlight tears the room.

My voice goes and loses me.

You know this like the back of your face.

I thought of burying myself behind the curve of the earth,—I was a little concerned about winding up right back here.

I saw the door and its shadow bang shut at the same time; or rather, I saw the door bang shut and saw its shadow disappear.

The whole process is presumptuous; for instance, why is it that I think that someone other than the painter is in the room with the picture's subject?

I believe in black and white, but here are colors free and real as ground-flung meat just under the leaves.

No phone, no lights, no motorcar.

Not a single apolitical comfort.

So, irretrievable, we took entire dreams to get here—the world is nearer than the living are alive.

Oh say it's just before brunch in America.

Oh say a gull shoves through knuckled fog.

There's been the beginning—drab buildings, dawdling heroes, gobs of light; there's been a grief in which only other grief made sense.

Sky that it is, the only sky up there's no one.

The last of the last of the rain will never make the gray trees.

I find my panicky kid in the garage, and I tell him, "That's just your other heart—I didn't mean to build it."

Same boy says, "Look at these scissors."

You understand that he says this by throwing them.

And why not wave at the ship?

History's all up in the lighthouse, the belfry.

My promise is fixing to rip its way back to the past.

Like any of the beautiful people, I'm flawed, though that's the only way in which I at all resemble said beautiful people, most of whom are off doing whatever it is that's worth doing wherever they are.

I think of them often and as a mountain of glass anvils.

I think of me sinking with a submarine's weird quiet.

It's that time again, time for someone—in this case, you—to hear a poem in which the speaker—in this case, me—makes use of phrases like "It's that time again" or "This is a test" or "This just in."

The beach is closed and ghostless; the houses throw their light out to the cold.

I want to die a way I used to—say, a great heart attack brought on by my mistaking the rustle of bush-caught plastic bags for some rabid animal—but no . . .

It's been a good year for the overrated waves.

Whole cloud, failed cloud.

Okay orchid, scream them petals.

Our very background is everywhere away.

Example: the tired slide to equity.

Example: my fathered-up vocabulary.

Example: a JPEG of a photo of a painting of the shadows of a river on the bottom of a leaf.

These woods without porno, whose are they?

At rest, the mouth's indefinite, maybe derogatory.

Oh go to light.

I move to touch me as if I were evidence.

The noon sun scorns the body forward, the day moon the mind.

Off I go loved into the Great Why Bother, into pieces like an obsolete blossom.

I'll be gentle when I'm dead.

I'm welcome.

The poem is the continuation of poetry by other means.

I look just beyond the rat's nest in my head at rich-kid city.

I zoom out a little once I see its bodies limp with sleep.

Every city flaunts its windows, hauls light into its rooms, hangs a uniform on anyone who'll point apart the sheep.

Tick and tick—the clock dispenses each and any second as if it's its first.

I keep my mouth to myself.

I put my brains where I can see them.

I've got my hands where I can make the poem worse.

These are the voyages of the starship Heartshake.

At what jokes does one balk?

At what speed should one leave?

These are the voyages of the starship Gum Disease.

I've come straight into the room as if the poem was to be for me, and what I meant was that the day moon dims to gauze.

It's remarkable too—or maybe it just seems like that—the way the sun can discover clear glass on the floor of a stream.

These are voyages of the starship Jug of Jim Beam.

I try to wreck myself useful, to cause rules to then leak from the game.

A wasp slaps the window, drones on, an habitual N.

These are the voyages of the starship Crock of Nerves.

These are the voyages of the starship Where've You Been?

Here the ghost goes talking with my teeth again, folks.

And does he move, refuse all shape.

Excuse me, but those of us whose bones aren't only rumors want a turn.

Of course a glitch is best and his is fixed.

Crust and mantle, core—the fuck else would the world be there for?

If ever dusk coughs up permission, yes, or if a loud and spastic squall should boss the field around, fine, but don't forget I lost the question.

Just scratch me a sea.

Just scratch a sea through this unending empty instant.

It is at times a mind is darker than its thought's believed-in bruise.

This fire gets into everything.

I'll go set the alarm for all night.

I don't mean to hate December.

The name for a feeling is another; moreover, some stranger has one's lover's very name.

Lying around in the library, ready, any patron has the right to say "I."

I sleep with my hands open.

The poem is a banjo in the foliage.

Thus far there's been blood but no bleeding, no orchard; the curve of a curve but no skin.

In the rhythm of these things, I have to stop without saying, remember songs I would've had to've been said to sing.

A lantern's lit, then in the river.

Short piers, hendecasyllabic walks from, 3–4, 41, 162n6.

Whatever's in my mouth is somehow loud to her.

Knowledge is by nature erotic—a guess is a kiss.

Let down your head, for whosoever can get around us and into the next fatality will.

The currency of poetry is ice.

Another holiday party begins: identical snowflakes, forty coats on a bed like a mound of abandoned skins.

I do so drink, misquote the host; I do so guzzle.

I shake off my face and then retch a small wind.

Good call on the famine.

Good call on those slices of lust.

Nice work on all the fiction—such classic mire, what immoderate din.

My throat's a muscle.

Taste my tongue for me.

Put your head in my upcoming grin.

Down's the data over which I'm always moving, underfed.

Up's the data under which I'm always moving.

There's everything I can do, but other gusts could change the subject.

Cradling what I'll crush, I'm keeping rampant in the yard's ungainly shade.

The building sways and so won't break.

The building sways and doesn't break.

The boy'll sleep all night and when he wakes I'll have a name for
him.

He'll rise to stack me full of ligament and sense.

I kneel in giant light, in no light, in the dumbest of what I don't say.

Oh and I lied before about being provided for.

I often up and greet the day with smears of egg.

Often I am permitted to return a few phone calls from a meadow.

That was then, this is then, which is to say that this is probably a movie.

I'm almost never in it, but I don't let that get to me.

I play the improbably dull stepchild in the stage version, you know.

And if the sets are cold and cluttered, at least two-thirds of the back-drops are lovely.

I weep the tears of a professional and ignore my unpaid understudy.

The day coagulates, and morning's cartoon warfare has me laughing myself in half.

Rumor has it its creator pulled those thousand-dollar cufflinks from the trash.

We all get intermittent blisters; we all have twentieth and twenty-first thoughts.

So what if I have to lug fake snow up to a catwalk and dump it.

Sometimes I open up my blood to find that blood is all I've got.

Different winter, actual river, every star carved through the dark.

The trees were filled with nothing and with moon.

My head was broken fruit, and who was I to dream in white.

And I'd been bleeding on a rare and borrowed book that I'd dreamt white.

Then, whatever love, whatever blood, a touch of lead; some lesser truth I kept dispatching back to color.

A glass of orange juice, too; a pen and pushpins—that's for summer.

And that's a vodka bottle full of quiet bees.

Alongside every velvet rope, there hung another, more velvety rope, and they were waiting for their chance to say, "You're never getting in."

Cursing into circuits, did I agree to a gentlemen's ending?

Sometimes it's only ever evening.

I lost all signal to a cold and shifting wind.

Sometimes it's only ever morning.

So much meat, so much clothing, so much wood, light, et cetera.

A remedial breeze is making everything change places.

The poem trails me not unlike a savior, an assailant.

There may be an excess even of informing day.

The boy plays alone by a loud blank creek.

I think that if I can just make it to the quiet parts or part I'll be okay.

The clouds fit together like porcelain.

The stars fit together like—what else?—your more typical stars.

For weeks I can wake to where I'm living and think that I'm hating it.

Sometimes I love being happy and in pain.

The world's whoever's in on it.

The poem was to be called "The Economy."

I'm the line between never and a very long wait.

It's not so much the cold as it is the economy.

I guessed at the blast; I thought up at the blue; and I discovered the poem to give it something to do.

Said poem can only be vandalized into focus.

Oh say the house is the bitterest ship and the frame of affection.

Oh say that sex is less a daydream than a fact.

I can only take requests for what I'm thinking when I'm thinking.

I almost called the poem "The New Humidity."

I almost called the poem "Paint It Back."

Spit if you will the picture, a coughed self-portrait—we live in the eye.

An idea's the wake of what?

I'm every word; the depth's no worse for it.

Call out the bottle, not the thought of it, the aim, the sorry fly.

Go forth and get that minor triumph over with, by which I mean just get on into the sky.

The fog's coming open.

What's a touch but a small explosion?

Where else but in some contraption like the grass?

Years, and the potentially two-dimensional hills still seem the same.

Oh say the scene dries up and into memory, amen.

Oh say that anything that doesn't isn't harmed.

I tend to envy the wealthy their ingots.

I tend to slather all weather with thought.

I tend toward long, illocal nightmares in which the sunsets are pigeon-eye orange.

When I imagine a valid me, I then imagine that that valid me is real.

I'm there to tell me: here I am under all that clarity.

But am I scratches on the present?

And would I've made the best dust?

I'd say I'm what you'd call remote with love.

My human rights are weird, as is that word on the worn-out ground;
as is the single speck of red—a fruit? a bird?—in the blurry orchard.

I've come straight into the room as if the poem was to be for me.

It leaves me just enough awake to hear it leave.

History makes nothing happen.

I wasn't prone to throwing dirt, but once upon a clean and shattered plate I called a face I did.

At its most real, which is not to say in its latest versions, what I've come to call who we are is just so much software.

Today the sun dug everyone up and disappeared.

It started to rain the same all over the place, and because I feared I was exactly who the poem didn't want me to be, I called for upgrades if not progress.

I could've arranged it so that the storm didn't soak open that recently-dropped-off FedEx box, but he—my double, my neighbor—was just so much better at it.

I thrilled to watch him leap into the street and wag his fist.

Later, at dinner, a temblor.

A from-out-of-town guest gasped, "What was *that*?"

I drained my usual ontological cocktail, a death and something.

I dragged a napkin toward my teeth and dropped it back.

Like the docent who would suck all hint of interest from his subject, I'll warn you now that I've been known to cheat at reverie.

I wake apart to dark, suggest a presence, some lone imagination gummed with time.

And still the city hides its sentence, a parade of strokes and serifs only weeds and piles of broken bricks derive.

Come daybreak, one more heat wave, an all-day hate crime in the sky.

And the kiss?

I got behind on it.

Do I know the drill?

I *am* the drill.

Or rather, I am until an hour of clumsy silences renders me otherwise.

I should pretend myself to sleep again.

A few more injuries are scheduled to arrive.

I could break into slavery, certain songs hung on my bones.

The poem: think to listen at me fix that.

I've come straight into the room as if the poem was to be for me.

Vague scraping at the shingles, vaguer flashing in the air—I get it.

S'all evil.

The poem is briars and bells of poison.

The torn half of a book is in the wine that's crawling toward me on the floor.

Has a hard, bright eye, today does, and with one fist and a finger in the world I've come to hell.

The poem peels its speech from me.

The revolution will probably be pantomimed.

The poem keeps away when I can't see or there's nothing to see.

The night in its stages, the day all at once, and then language detaches into slow laughs, actually, while memory drains the path.

How'm I cracking?

Have I sung?

The first thing into the bag's the box it came in, son, so be honest, keep shopping.

I don't know from the poem, from these sounds I've always had and never will.

When I end and they begin, there comes a light in the mind like vi-
olence.

You could cut me with a rained-out cigarette.

I'm decanting these eyes into those hands.

I'll get old, I suppose, and never know not to rage at paper.

I'll burn to but a germ—what won't so black a story smother?

There's a violence in the mind like light.

Another noon—for that much time has in fact elapsed—feeds back above the previous grasses.

I thought that by now I'd've simply relaxed into a sort of deformity.

To that end, I've come straight into the room in which the poem was to be for me.

This is just to point and gape, to be so forgotten as to knock on my own door.

I've been asked to say a few words in a voice like tin on tin, to draft excuses on our burgeoning behalf.

This just in: framing devices, flower devices—the ready garden and our other pretty failures tell us little.

Exactly what have I been heaving past my lips to make you laugh?

Some rabid amateurs watch a cloud through which no aircraft ever screams.

The rain is down.

New stars will out.

Another hell is where I tell them what this means.

Life in, life out—think it off.

What don't I do for a living?

I don't do earfuls of obstacle.

I don't do value pangs.

I don't crawl in among the flags and dead adversaries.

In a far, cruel future, they'll threaten to comfort me, though.

They'll tuck my head in a quake-deranged ocean.

I'll fill with everything I'll never need to know.

A new sign in the food court restroom requests I use only the resources I need.

Those are French fries on the stairs.

There's a syllable tears through me like joy.

We have the right to a more festive discharge.

We have the right to recalibrate the labyrinth.

A dead leaf has a degree of specificity that a gun to my face is unable to share with it.

Bring on the jerkwater verbiage, the wrestlers in pairs.

Two branches click together.

And Life is over there— / Behind the shelf.

My words aren't half misguided if they're music to my teeth.

They're parts of thought like any others, draped in leisure.

I drag the poem through a heart that would explode in its own image.

I'm coming straight into the room.)

Stay figure.

ACKNOWLEDGMENTS Thanks to the following editors for publishing sentences from this book: Chris Hosea and Cecily Iddings of *The Blue Letter*, Ben Lerner of *Critical Quarterly*, Ben Mirov of *LIT*, Daniela Olszewska of *Black Warrior Review*, and D. A. Powell and T. J. DiFrancesco of *Lo-Ball*. § Thanks to Ben Estes and Alan Felsenthal of The Song Cave for publishing "To Graham Foust on the Morning of His Fortieth Birthday" as a chapbook. § Thanks to Barbara Claire Freeman of Minus A Press for publishing "To Anacreon in Heaven" as a limited-edition book. Thanks also to Jeff Clark for his thoughtful design and composition of that edition (and of this one), as well as to The Millay Colony for the Arts and the Wallace Foundation, without whom the writing of the poem would not have been possible. § This book owes much to Geoffrey G. O'Brien's parsings and good advices.

GRAHAM FOUST is the author of four previous books of poetry, including *A Mouth in California* (Flood Editions, 2009). With Samuel Frederick, he is also the translator of Ernst Meister's *In Time's Rift* (Wave Books, 2012). He teaches in the English department at University of Denver.